# Pokémon™
## Book of
# Evolutions

**Written by Katherine Andreou**

DK

# Contents

# Welcome!

It's time to explore the exciting world of Pokémon Evolutions! Here, you'll learn everything there is to know about the amazing ways Pokémon can evolve and the mysterious items that help them. Meet Evolutionary experts, top Trainers, and tons of epic Pokémon!

# All About Evolution

# What is Evolution?

Pokémon don't always stay the same forever. For some, there is an exciting journey of change ahead!

## A new start

The more time a Pokémon spends training in battle, the stronger it will become. Eventually, most will level up, which means they evolve into their next form. They may gain a new name, look, or Pokémon type.

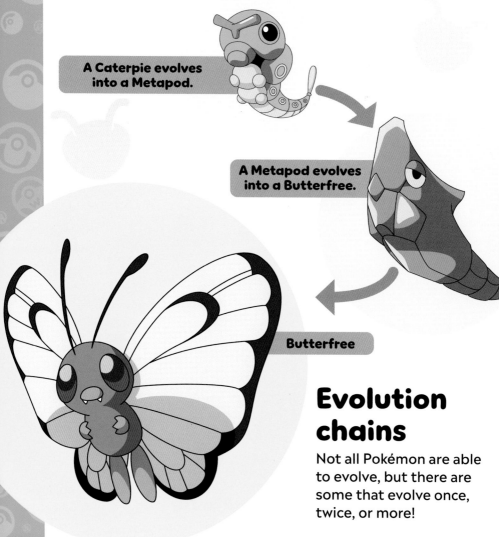

A Caterpie evolves into a Metapod.

A Metapod evolves into a Butterfree.

Butterfree

## Evolution chains

Not all Pokémon are able to evolve, but there are some that evolve once, twice, or more!

# How to evolve

While most Pokémon level up to evolve, some might need to learn a certain move, find a certain item, or form a strong friendship with their Trainer. Some even need to wait for the right weather condition in order to evolve!

Sliggoo evolves only during foggy or rainy weather.

# Multiple forms

Some Pokémon have lots of forms they are able to evolve into. Rockruff can change into one of three forms of Lycanroc, depending on the time of day it evolves.

Midday Form Lycanroc

Midnight Form Lycanroc

Rockruff

Dusk Form Lycanroc

# Squirtle's Evolution

**From tiny tackler to blasting battler, see how Squirtle evolves!**

Stubby arms

Hard shell protects it from danger

**Squirtle**

Ears help with balance during swimming

Furry tail

**Wartortle**

Powerful rocket cannons can fire water

**Blastoise**

Short, pointed tail

## Did you know?

**Blastoise's huge rocket cannons fire jets of water so strong they can rip through thick steel!**

# Why evolve your Pokémon?

**You might think your Pokémon are perfect—but evolving them could be even better.**

## Complete your Pokédex

If you've got goals like Goh, evolving your Pokémon can be a huge help in filling up your Pokédex. Especially when it comes to those tricky to find Pokémon, like Flygon.

Pokémon Trainer Goh and his Pokédex

### Did you know?

A Pokédex is an electronic tool that stores Pokémon facts and stats.

Flygon

Trapinch's Evolution, Flygon, can be hard to find in the wild!

Corvisquire

# Make Pokémon more powerful

Evolved Pokémon have access to more moves and can sometimes gain an extra type.

Corviknight

Flying-type Corvisquire becomes Corviknight, a Flying- and Steel-type, when it evolves.

# Get a battle bonus

If Growlithe is struggling to defeat a Pokémon, then evolving into the heavier Arcanine might make it able to beat its opponent more easily.

Growlithe

Arcanine

Arcanine is 299 lb heavier than Growlithe.

# Evolutionary experts

**Throughout the regions, there are Trainers with a special interest in Evolution. They love to share their knowledge!**

## Professor Rowan

Evolution expert Professor Rowan has studied Pokémon for years. He often uses his own Starly and Staraptor for his research.

Starly

Professor Rowan

Staraptor

Steven Stone

## Steven Stone

Steven's last name is a good clue to what he's interested in—he is on a mission to uncover Evolution Stones! He is also very interested in Mega Evolution.

# Gurkinn

Gurkinn's distant ancestors were the first Trainers ever to Mega Evolve a Pokémon. This is the process by which a Pokémon becomes bigger and stronger in battle.

Gurkinn

# Korrina

Gym Leader Korrina is Gurkinn's granddaughter. She'd like him to teach her everything he knows about Pokémon Evolution.

Korrina is determined to Mega Evolve her beloved Pokémon, Lucario.

Professor Sycamore

# Professor Sycamore

A leading expert in Mega Evolution, Professor Sycamore loves caring for Pokémon. He likes to travel across many regions to conduct his exciting research. His good friend, Garchomp, is always by his side.

Garchomp

# Pokémon Eggs

You can find Pokémon Eggs in an Egg Nursery—or you might even spot one in the wild. What a cracking start to an Evolution journey!

Ash found a Pokémon Egg that later hatched into Togepi.

Togepi

## What are Pokémon Eggs?

Some Pokémon have the ability to breed and create Pokémon Eggs. Some of these Eggs go on to hatch into Pokémon.

Happiny carries around a white rock that it believes is an Egg!

# Pokémon Egg Raisers

In the Hoenn region, May and Ash visited an Egg Nursery. Here, people called Pokémon Egg Raisers keep many Eggs safe in their care.

# Epic Egg patterns

Sometimes the pattern on the outside of an Egg matches the look of the Pokémon inside. The Egg that contained Lillie's Alolan Vulpix, Snowy, was icy-colored and beautiful, just like Snowy herself!

**Snowy's Egg**

**Snowy**

# Happy hatches

While Eggs don't count as their own Evolution stage, they can spark the beginning of a baby Pokémon's journey into the world. Once hatched, many of them require max friendship to evolve.

**To evolve into Lucario, Riolu will need max friendship with its Trainer.**

# Legendary Evolution

While most Legendary Pokémon have no Evolution chain, there are some exciting exceptions. The mysterious Cosmog can transform into two Legendary Pokémon!

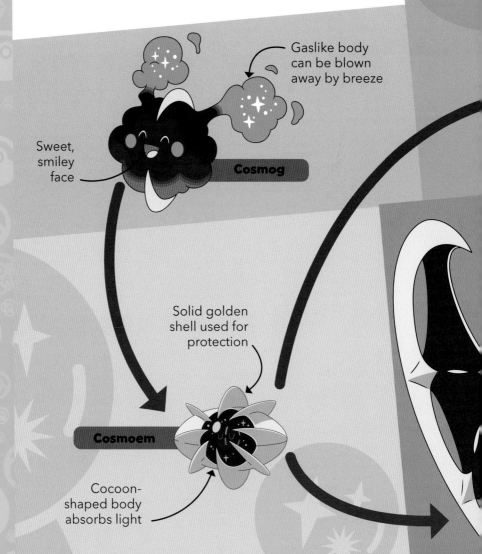

Gaslike body can be blown away by breeze

Sweet, smiley face

Cosmog

Solid golden shell used for protection

Cosmoem

Cocoon-shaped body absorbs light

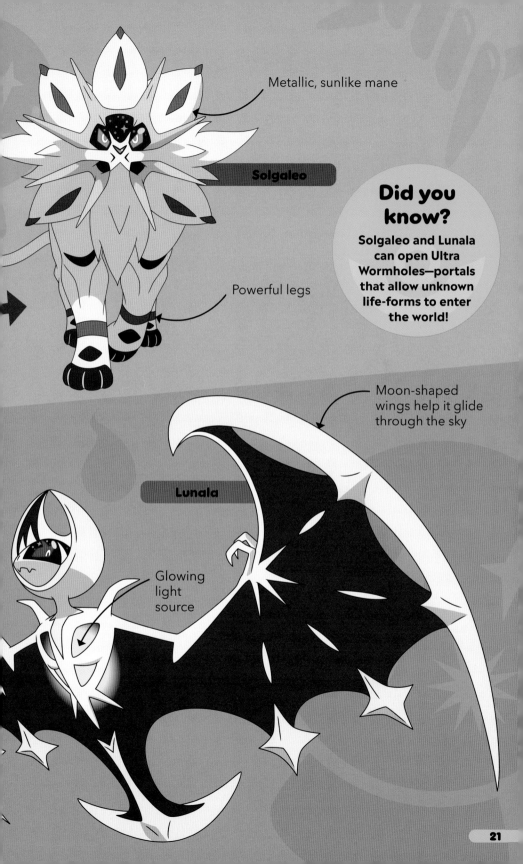

Metallic, sunlike mane

**Solgaleo**

Powerful legs

## Did you know?

Solgaleo and Lunala can open Ultra Wormholes—portals that allow unknown life-forms to enter the world!

Moon-shaped wings help it glide through the sky

**Lunala**

Glowing light source

# To evolve... or not?

Many Pokémon are excited by the idea of evolving. But there are others who are not so sure.

**Ash**

**Pikachu**

## Ash's Pikachu

Ash's proud Pikachu wants to prove himself a strong competitor without changing a thing. He ran away when another Pikachu tried to give him a Thunder Stone to help him evolve.

Ash's Pikachu won't take the Thunder Stone.

Rowlet is about to eat the Everstone!

## Ash's Rowlet

Silly Rowlet may have wanted to evolve, but it swallowed an item called an Everstone, thinking it was food! An Everstone stops a Pokémon from ever evolving.

# Team Rocket's Meowth

Team Rocket's Meowth is unique in many ways. Not only can it walk and talk like a human, but it also refuses to evolve.

**James**

**Jessie**

**Meowth**

## A bitter rivalry

Why does Meowth refuse to evolve into Persian? Some say it's because it dislikes the Persian belonging to Team Rocket boss, Giovanni.

**Lillie**

**Snowy**

# Lillie's Alolan Vulpix

Lillie asked her Alolan Vulpix, Snowy, if it wanted to evolve using an item called an Ice Stone. Snowy was scared, so refused.

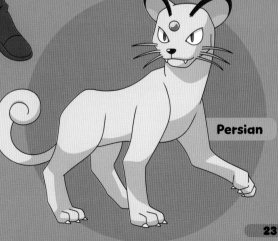

**Persian**

# Pokémon with no Evolutions

More than 100 Pokémon have no currently known pre-Evolutions or Evolutions at all. Here are just a few of them...

Pachirisu

Ditto

Mimikyu

Comfey

Morpeko
(Full Belly Mode)

Morpeko
(Hangry Mode)

Morpeko doesn't evolve. But when it gets hungry—it gets angry!

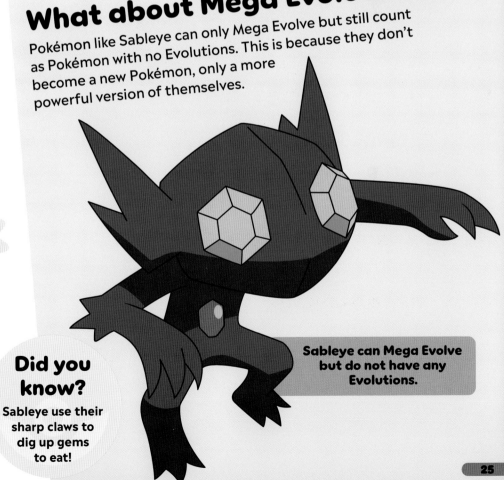

# What about Mega Evolutions?

Pokémon like Sableye can only Mega Evolve but still count as Pokémon with no Evolutions. This is because they don't become a new Pokémon, only a more powerful version of themselves.

## Did you know?

Sableye use their sharp claws to dig up gems to eat!

Sableye can Mega Evolve but do not have any Evolutions.

# Epic Evolutions

# Awesome Eevee

**With eight currently known Evolutions, Eevee is not called the Evolution Pokémon for nothing!**

Eevee can change shape, size, and type. Its sensitivity to its surroundings allow it to adapt smoothly to any setting. But once it evolves, it cannot evolve again.

Large brown ears

Bushy tail

Furry collar

Soft feet

# Battling Brothers

Rainer, Sparky, and Pyro use special stones to evolve Eevee. A Water Stone yields Vaporeon, a Thunder Stone gives Jolteon, and a Fire Stone evolves Flareon.

# To the Rescue!

The Pokémon Rescue Squad is dedicated to helping others. Eevee, as well as all of Eevee's evolutions, are part of the dream team.

# Eevee Lab

At the Eevee Evolution Laboratory, the Researchers are kept busy investigating how Eevee evolves— or occasionally doesn't evolve!

Flareon

Vaporeon

Leafeon

Sylveon

Glaceon

Umbreon

Jolteon

Espeon

# Males and females

**The gender of your Pokémon can play a big part in how they will evolve.** It can also change the way a Pokémon looks.

Kirlia

Gardevoir evolve from a female Kirlia.

## Big changes

Pokémon like Kirlia, Snorunt, and Burmy are able to evolve into two completely different Pokémon depending on their gender.

Gallade evolve from a male Kirlia.

# Tiny tweaks

There are few noticeable differences between some male and female Pokémon. For Pikachu, you just need to look at their tails! The female's tail is heart-shaped, while the male's tail is a thunderbolt shape.

**Ash's Pikachu meets a female friend in Pikachu Valley.**

**Froslass evolve from a female Snorunt.**

**Snorunt**

**Glalie evolve from a male Snorunt.**

# Changing types

Many Pokémon keep their types throughout Evolution. However, some are lucky enough to gain or even switch type as they evolve.

**Pancham**
Type: Fighting

**Pangoro**
Type: Fighting-Dark

**Shelgon**
Type: Dragon

**Salamence**
Type: Dragon-Flying

# Special switches

Aside from Eevee, only two other Pokémon are currently known to entirely change types when they evolve.

**In the Alola region, Ground-type Cubone evolves into Fire- and Ghost-type, Alolan Marowak.**

**Cubone**
Type: Ground

**Alolan Marowak**
Type: Fire-Ghost

**In the Galar region, Water- and Rock-type Corsola evolves into Ghost-type Cursola.**

**Corsola**
Type: Water-Rock

**Cursola**
Type: Ghost

# Fun to fierce

It's hard to believe, but some sweet Pokémon can evolve into a really scary squad!

Sweet Phanpy evolves into tough Donphan.

Donphan

## Extra force

Some Pokémon may get overlooked—until they evolve into another fantastic form. Whismur's cries can give you a headache. But the thundering shouts of Exploud can be heard across whole cities!

Exploud

Whismur

# First partner Evolutions

The final Evolutions of these first partners from the Sinnoh region are enough to make anyone nervous before battle!

Empoleon's sharp wings can slice ice.

Piplup

Infernape is quick to attack enemies.

Chimchar

Torterra weighs a fearsome 683.4 lb.

Turtwig

# Charmander's Evolution

**Fiery Charmander turns up the heat each time it evolves!**

Large blue eyes

Fire-tipped tail, always burns bright

**Charmander**

One blunt horn

**Charmeleon**

Super-sharp claws ready for attack

**Did you know?**

It is believed that Charizard's fire burns hotter if it has fought in harsh battles in the past.

Charizard

Fierce face in battle

Huge wings help it fly fast

# Regional Evolutions

If you travel across the Pokémon world, you might spot exciting regional Evolutions! These are different forms of Pokémon that are special to one location.

## New region, new look

Each regional Evolution looks different to their usual form. While Ponyta usually has a fiery mane to match its type, in the Galar region, it takes on a more magical look.

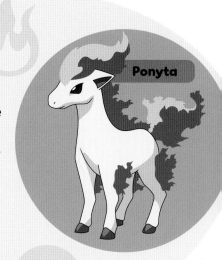

Ponyta

Galarian Ponyta

Alolan Raichu

## Type changes

Most regional Evolutions also gain another type. In the Alola region, Pikachu might evolve into an Alolan Raichu—becoming an awesome Electric- and Psychic-type!

# All-new Evolutions

While Mr. Mime cannot evolve in most regions, in the Galar region, it evolves into an entirely new Pokémon called Mr. Rime.

Galarian
Mr. Mime

Mr. Rime

# Multiple forms

Meowth has more than one regional Evolution. Alolan Meowth can evolve into Alolan Persian in the Alola region. But in Galar, a Galarian Meowth evolves into a whole new Pokémon called Perrserker.

Alolan Persian

Perrserker

# Little to large

When some Pokémon evolve, they grow in size. They might look instantly stronger thanks to their growth spurt!

## A bigger battle

Pokémon can sometimes evolve during a battle. Seeing one of these massive Evolutions all of a sudden can be quite a shock!

### Did you know?

Munchlax and Snorlax love eating food so much—they don't even care if it's rotten!

| | |
|---|---|
| **Sobble**<br>Height: 1' 00"<br>Weight: 8.8 lb | **Inteleon**<br>Height: 6' 03"<br>Weight: 99.6 lb |

9 ft
8 ft
7 ft
6 ft
5 ft
4 ft
3 ft
2 ft
1 ft
0 ft

| | |
|---|---|
| **Munchlax**<br>Height: 2' 00"<br>Weight: 231.5 lb | **Snorlax**<br>Height: 6' 11"<br>Weight: 1014.1 lb |

# Small but mighty

You might be surprised that bigger Pokémon aren't always better. There are plenty of little Pokémon who pack a lot of power. Even a tiny Morelull, or its Evolution, Shiinotic, have the potential to take down a Beartic!

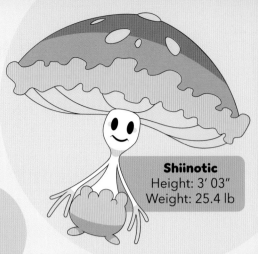

**Shiinotic**
Height: 3' 03"
Weight: 25.4 lb

**Morelull**
Height: 0' 08"
Weight: 3.3 lb

**Cubchoo**
Height: 1' 08"
Weight: 18.7 lb

**Beartic**
Height: 8' 06"
Weight: 573.2 lb

# Size shrinkers

While many Pokémon grow larger as they evolve, some get smaller in size. Just look at this little lot!

## Tall to small

Don't let their shorter height fool you—Pokémon with smaller Evolutions can still pack a punch!

**Haunter**
Height: 5' 03"

**Gengar**
Height: 4' 11"

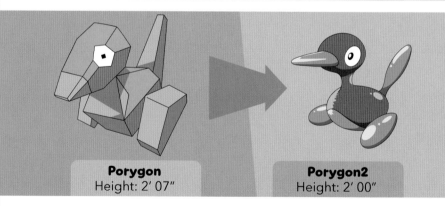

**Porygon**
Height: 2' 07"

**Porygon2**
Height: 2' 00"

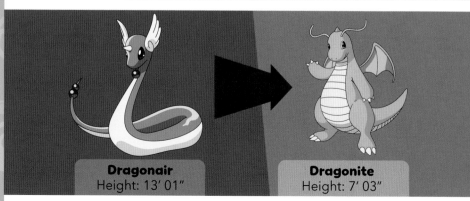

**Dragonair**
Height: 13' 01"

**Dragonite**
Height: 7' 03"

# Heavy to light

These lightweight fighters know how to use their weight to their advantage. It can help them move more quickly and carefully.

**Bellossom**
Weight: 12.8 lb

**Gloom**
Weight: 19.0 lb

**Alakazam**
Weight: 105.8 lb

**Kadabra**
Weight: 124.6 lb

**Shedinja**
Weight: 2.6 lb

**Nincada**
Weight: 12.1 lb

# Unique Evolutions

**Starting from friendships—or even fights—some Pokémon Evolutions are pretty special!**

## Fierce fighters

Tyrogue has three possible Evolutions—Hitmonlee, Himonchan, and Hitmontop. Which one it evolves into depends on how strong its attack and defense are.

### Did you know?

Hitmonlee is known for its crushing kicks, while Hitmonchan is famous for its power punches!

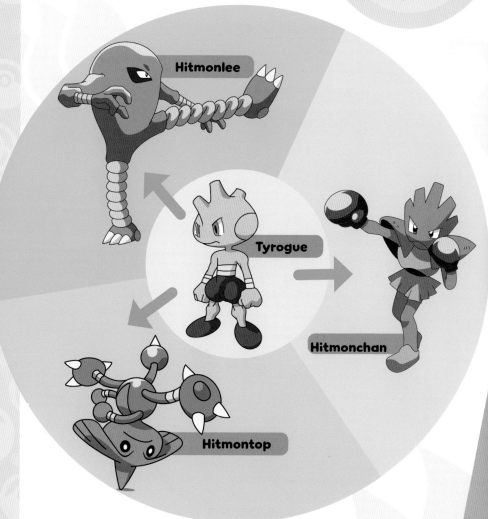

Hitmonlee

Tyrogue

Hitmonchan

Hitmontop

# Personality matters

Wurmple evolves into either Silcoon or Cascoon depending on its personality. Since this information is hidden from its Trainer, they won't know what they're going to get until it evolves!

Silcoon

Wurmple

Cascoon

# Bonded besties

Mantyke are known to swim alongside a school of Remoraid, often teaming up to fend off attackers. So, it's no surprise that Mantyke can only evolve into Mantine when a Remoraid is in its Trainer's team.

Remoraid

Mantyke

# Evolution Power-Ups

# Evolution Items

From strawberry sweets to Evolution stones—there are lots of cool items a Trainer can use to help their Pokémon evolve.

## Held items

Some Pokémon are given a special item to hold by their Trainer. This, along with certain conditions, can cause their Evolution.

A Slowpoke holding the item King's Rock evolved into Slowking when it was traded to a different Trainer.

Slowking

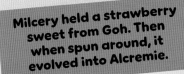

### Did you know?

Alcremie has 70 forms. Which one Milcery evolves into depends on which sweet it is holding.

Milcery held a strawberry sweet from Goh. Then when spun around, it evolved into Alcremie.

Alcremie

Ash gave Gligar a Razor Fang. If it levels up at night while holding it, it will evolve into Gliscor.

Gliscor

Gligar

# Instant items

Items like Evolution stones can make some Pokémon evolve right away. There are currently 10 different Evolution stones, including Fire Stone, Water Stone, and Thunder Stone. If you want a Sunflora, you'll need a Sun Stone!

Sunflora

Sunkern evolved into Sunflora using a Sun Stone given to it by Ash.

# Remarkable locations

Sometimes a Pokémon needs to be at a particular location for it to evolve. From hidden gardens to busy towns, all these places have a mystical power that helps Pokémon to transform into a new form.

## Trapinch Underground Lake

Within a rocky desert is the Trapinch Underground Labyrinth. Beneath the Labyrinth there is a lake where Trapinch can evolve into Vibrava.

## Evolution Mountain

This mighty peak is famous for its stones that trigger Evolution. At its base is Stone Town, where many Pokémon, including Shellder, transform.

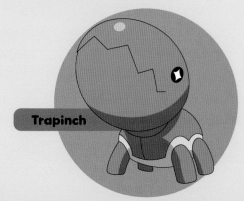

Trapinch

Shellder

# Poni Canyon

Poni Canyon is a deep ravine that leads to the mysterious Altar of the Sunne. This area has a magnetic field that helps Charjabug to evolve.

# Geosenge Town

Famous for its caves and unique Evolution Stones, Geosenge Town is where Trainer Korrina Mega Evolves Lucario into Mega Lucario.

Mega Lucario

Charjabug

# Mysterious Garden

This mystical garden appears only when there is a Bulbasaur Evolution festival. The ceremony is led by Bulbasaur's final form, Venusaur.

Bulbasaur

# Dynamax power

This brilliant battle tool was first introduced in the Galar region. It's hugely exciting!

Ash was able to Dynamax his Gengar during training.

## What is Dynamax?

Dynamax is a battle feature where Trainers use a Dynamax Band to encourage their Pokémon to become larger and stronger versions of themselves.

A Dynamax Band is worn around Ash's wrist.

## Watch out!

In the wild, Dynamax Pokémon behave differently. They might lose control and go on a rampage!

This Dynamax Snorlax blocked a railroad line and terrified all the nearby Wooloo.

# Why Dynamax?

When Dynamaxed, Pokémon perform special Max Moves. A Water-type like Gyarados is given the Water-type move Max Geyser.

Lance's shiny Dynamax Gyarados used its Max Geyser move on Leon's Charizard at the World Coronation Series.

## Gigantamax greatness

Gigantamax is a type of Dynamax where Pokémon grow huge and change forms. They are able to use G-Max moves, which are even stronger than Max Moves!

Team Rocket weren't too excited to meet Gigantamax Drednaw!

## Who can Gigantamax?

Currently, just over 30 Pokémon are able to Gigantamax, including Pikachu, Eevee, and Lapras.

Pikachu

# Mega Evolution

Mega Evolution is a powerful battle tool that first appeared in the Kalos region.

## How to Mega Evolve

To Mega Evolve a Pokémon, a Trainer must have an item called a Key Stone, as well as a special stone unique to that Pokémon. For example, Ampharos require an Ampharosite stone to Mega Evolve.

**Ampharosite**

**Mega Ampharos**

### Battle buddies

The Trainer can Mega Evolve their Pokémon only during battle. Once the battle has finished, the Pokémon will return to its normal form.

**Ampharos**

## Duo form Pokémon

Currently only two Pokémon—Charizard and Mewtwo—can Mega Evolve into two different forms.

**Charizard**

# Why Mega Evolve?

Not only does Mega Evolving make your Pokémon stronger and faster, but it also gives them an awesome new look!

Houndoom

Houndoomite

Mega Houndoom

## Who can Mega Evolve?

More than 40 Pokémon can Mega Evolve, including Gyarados and Garchomp. Once a Pokémon has Mega Evolved, its name changes. For example, Houndoom becomes Mega Houndoom.

Charizardite X

Mega Charizard X

Charizardite Y

**Charizard X is a Fire- and Dragon-type, while Charizard Y is a Fire- and Flying-type. It's completely up to the Trainer which one they choose!**

Mega Charizard Y

# Bulbasaur's Mega Evolution

**Watch Bulbasaur bloom into its mega, final Evolution!**

Bulbasaur

Plant seed that stores nutrients

Wide smile

Pink bud grows larger in sunlight

Lush leaves

Ivysaur

## Did you know?

**Venusaur stay on the move to seek sunlight. Solar energy helps their plant bloom.**

**Mega Venusaur is bigger and stronger than Venusaur.**

Large flower that can release a calming smell

**Venusaur**

Short, sturdy legs

# Fantastic friendship

A strong bond between Pokémon and Trainer can cause a Pokémon to evolve—sometimes with perfect timing!

Noivern

Noibat

## Ash's Noivern

When Ash's Noibat saw its teammate Hawlucha falling off a cliff, it evolved into Noivern to gain enough extra speed to save it.

## Serena's Sylveon

In a battle against Inkay and Slurpuff, Eevee used the power of its friendship with Serena, to help it evolve into Sylveon. This gave it the extra strength it needed to protect teammate Pikachu!

Sylveon and Serena

Team Rocket with Koffing and Ekans

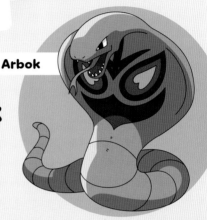

Arbok

# Team Rocket's Weezing and Arbok

Koffing and Ekans didn't want to evolve, until they noticed Team Rocket crying at the thought of losing them! When they realized how much Jessie and James cared, they finally evolved into Weezing and Arbok.

Chansey, Dawn, and Brock helped some poorly baby Pokémon feel better.

Pichu

# Brock's Chansey

Brock's Happiny evolved into Chansey so it could learn a healing move called Soft-Boiled. It was then able to help cure Pichu, who had been poisoned by a Tentacruel. This kindness inspired Brock to become a doctor.

**Project Editor** Lara Hutcheson
**Designers** Thelma-Jane Robb, James McKeag
**Senior Production Editor** Jennifer Murray
**Senior Production Controller** Lloyd Robertson
**Managing Editor** Paula Regan
**Managing Art Editor** Jo Connor
**Managing Director** Mark Searle

DK would like to thank Hank Woon and the rest of the team at
The Pokémon Company International. Thanks also to Jennette ElNaggar for
Americanization and proofreading, and Selina Wood for editorial assistance.
.
First American Edition, 2024
Published in the United States by DK Publishing
1745 Broadway, 20th Floor, New York, NY 10019

Page design copyright © 2024 Dorling Kindersley Limited
DK, a Division of Penguin Random House LLC
24 25 26 27 28 10 9 8 7 6 5 4 3 2 1
001–341327–July/2024

A catalog record for this book
is available from the Library of Congress.
ISBN 978-0-5938-4387-1

DK books are available at special discounts when purchased
in bulk for sales promotions, premiums, fund-raising, or educational use.
For details, contact: DK Publishing Special Markets,
1745 Broadway, 20th Floor, New York, NY 10019
SpecialSales@dk.com

Printed and bound in China

**www.dk.com**

MIX
Paper | Supporting
responsible forestry
FSC™ C018179

This book was made with Forest
Stewardship Council™ certified
paper – one small step in DK's
commitment to a sustainable future.
**Learn more at www.dk.com/uk/
information/sustainability**

Noibat

Rowlet

Galarian Ponyta

Pichu

Pikachu